The Book of Blunders

The Blook of Bunders

Waxing philosophic, Art Linkletter once said, "The road of life is strewn with the banana peels of embarrassment." How true. Here is proof from Art's abundant collection of foibles and faux pas.

Linkletter's Best Blunders

One of the greatest catastrophes that ever happened to me in public occurred when I was presiding at a very large dinner in a downtown Los Angeles hotel for one of the first coast-to-coast "Emmy" Award programs. Everybody was being so formal and pompous amid the smell of mothballs from rented tuxedos. I was introduced, walked out on stage, and just as I said, "Good evening, ladies and gentlemen," the master light switch exploded and plunged the hall into darkness. Stagehands began running in all directions, knocking the entire Grecian set down. Walls, pillars, and great facades tumbled onto the orchestra. One entire section of strings was knocked out by an enormous pillar. When the lights came on again and order was slowly restored, I stood calmly looking out over the wreckage, and instead of making everyone even more embarrassed by trying to apologize or explain, I said, "For an encore, ladies and gentlemen, we will now set fire to Lucille Ball."

Another dinner at the world-famous Cocoanut Grove in Los Angeles honored the president of a very large university. He was to come to the microphone and pick up an award, then walk over and present it to his wife. He was wired for sound with a small portable short-wave microphone transmitter, wires running down his pants and batteries in his back pocket. This gadgetry was to carry his voice from a microphone in his lapel to a backstage receiver for relaying to the audience through a public address speaker. But as he walked toward his wife, his sending set somehow became a radio receiver, as sometimes can happen. Suddenly over the public address system, straight from the man's back pocket, came a dignified commanding voice, "When you want a *real* fertilizer, get Vigoro!"...

Some of my favorite stories of embarrassing situations have become classics, such as the one about the young lady who had hay fever. Before going to a formal dinner party, she stuffed some handkerchiefs down her bosom just in case she began sneezing. Sure enough, she did. By the time dessert arrived, she was very intent on fumbling about in her bodice, fishing for another handkerchief. Looking up for an instant, she was terribly flustered to see that all eyes were upon her, so she blurted out, "Well, I know I had *two* when I

6

came in."...

A lady who had been after her husband for months to install a garbage disposal under the kitchen sink finally trapped him one Saturday afternoon, and he glumly got to work with his wrenches. Not wishing to listen to his colorful vocabulary as he banged his thumbs, she went out shopping. While downtown she ran into some girl friends and had a few cocktails, so she was feeling very friendly when she returned home. There was good old George still under the sink, working away, legs sticking out into the kitchen. So she bent down, reached under, and gave him a rudely familiar tweak. "Hi, honey," she said. There was a howl of surprise from under the sink as the man raised up and smacked his forehead against the disposal. It was the plumber! Her husband had given up on the job. The plumber crawled out, his forehead all bloody, and the wife ran to phone for an ambulance. The husband helped the attendant load the poor plumber onto a stretcher. "How'd it happen?" asked the attendant as they were carrying the man out. When the husband told him, the attendant began laughing so hard he let go of the stretcher — and the plumber plunged to the sidewalk, breaking his arm. Imagine explaining that one to the insurance company.

Jane Wyman Threatens Murder

Beautiful Jane Wyman, talented actress and accomplished hostess, pleads guilty to first degree blooperism. Just before a very swank evening party, she pinned a note to her husband on the guest towels — "IF YOU USE THESE I WILL MURDER YOU." In the pre-party excitement she forgot about the note. Afterwards, to her dismay, she discovered the towels in perfect order, as well as the note itself. It was probably Jane's most embarrassing moment, but the guests didn't mind — they were probably glad to escape with their lives.

Prurient Interest 101

When Lord Longford, England's antismut champion, landed at the London airport, he was held by customs officials for bringing dirty books into the country. Only after his lordship indignantly explained that the books were for study purposes was he allowed to enter.

Sign on side of building: "Visit Our Bargain Basement — One Flight Up."

Early television was full of blunders. One dramatic scene showed a couple walking home in a snowstorm. When they entered their posh Manhattan apartment and sat down to tea, no one thought to turn off the snow. Pretty hard to carry on a normal conversation when there's a blizzard in your living room! Here, John Shanley gives us more reasons why television is sometimes called "The Light That Failed."

The Light That Failed

...Bloopers, boners and assorted goofs occur in radio and television periodically, in spite of determined efforts to stamp them out. It is on live TV

9

especially that the spectacular misadventures occur, providing sardonic enjoyment for viewers and horror for producers, directors and players.

Thus, on one crime program, after a murder had been shown, the actor who portrayed the corpse assumed — imprudently — that he was out of sight, arose and walked off the set. His unscheduled revivification was captured on camera and observed by viewers all over the country.

Stage fright can also play a part. During a lavish medieval banquet scene on TV, a live camera turned toward a splendidly accoutered herald. According to plan, he was to sound a fanfare, signaling the arrival at the feast of a group of nobles. The performer — an inexperienced fellow — raised a trumpet to his lips and suddenly was overcome with terror. He managed to produce a small, tooting sound and then sagged to the stage in a swoon....

For one of her Sunday night shows, Dinah Shore had rehearsed a song in which she, Bob Cummings and Gale Storm were scheduled, in the closing bars, to sit together on a bench. Between the last rehearsal and the actual telecast a different bench was substituted — one that, unlike the bench used in rehearsal, had no back. When the number was televised, the three performers sat down, leaned back and disappeared.

Some viewers thought it was an unusually lively finale.

Jack Paar, on his late night show, was doing a commercial for a headache remedy. He had trouble removing two of the advertised tablets from their bottle. The audience was amused when he filled the bottle with water, took a swig of it, capped the bottle and put it aside. Twenty minutes later there was a small explosion; pressure generated within the bottle had caused the top to pop off. Paar was understandably startled, and the audience roared.

A telecast from a race track once provided a merry *non sequitur* when the jockey who rode the winning horse in a major race was brought before the camera for a few words. Chris Schenkel, the announcer on this occasion, asked the jockey to tell just how he had won. Flushed with success, the victor began to talk.

But instead of answering the question, he started voicing a testimonial on behalf of the program's sponsor. His eyes had wandered in the direction of some commercial cue cards behind the camera. They were to be used at the close of the telecast. The jockey assumed that he had been provided with a convenient script. Mr. Schenkel interrupted him quickly and steered him back to the proper conversational course.

Betsy Palmer, one of the medium's more photogenic and talented actresses, also became involved in confusion related to a sporting event. During an appearance on the "Today" program, she was called upon to give the scores and highlights of the preceding day's baseball games.

Baseball is a subject to which Miss Palmer has devoted a minimum of attention. But she went along without difficulty until she reported that "Minnie" Minoso, the rugged outfielder of the Cleveland Indians, had driven in four runs with several extra base hits. Miss Palmer, realizing that this must be an achievement of merit, departed from the script to exclaim enthusiastically: "Good going, Minnie girl!"

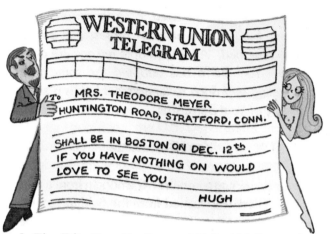

WESTERN UNION TELEGRAM

To MRS. THEODORE MEYER
HUNTINGTON ROAD, STRATFORD, CONN.

SHALL BE IN BOSTON ON DEC. 12th.
IF YOU HAVE NOTHING ON WOULD
LOVE TO SEE YOU.

HUGH

In The Fifty-Year Decline and Fall of Hollywood, *Ezra Goodman recounts the saga of a Hollywood publicist consigned to an ironic and unjust fate.*

Bird Brain

A Hollywood...classic has to do with an ingenious publicist at Paramount who, in 1934, devised an unusual publicity stunt for a Mae West movie, *It Ain't No Sin.* He put a platoon of parrots in a room with a phonograph record that kept playing the name of the picture over and over. After a while, the publicist had fifty or so parrots who would say *It Ain't No Sin* on cue. There was just one hitch. At the last minute the studio retitled the picture *I'm No Angel.*

"There has never been anyone else quite like her in America," says Alvin Harlow, "and Cincinnati, for one, hopes there never will be again." The person in question was Marion Devereux, social arbiter and society columnist for the Cincinnati Enquirer. *Cleveland Amory tells her story.*

Arbitrary Arbiter

In Marion Devereux, the strange and wonderful world of Society-page language soared to heights never before seen or attempted to be read. At the height of the Cincinnati "Season," a single weekday's social news would, in the tender hands of Miss Devereux, be accorded sixteen full columns, or two pages — and never was so much as a comma permitted to be changed....

And, of course, because of the style, there were the inevitable, albeit unintended, *doubles entendres.* Often they were extremely embarrassing to the entire staff of the paper, but, again of course, not a word could be changed:

Mr. and Mrs. Tom Conroy have been the center of many merry moments since their return from their honeymoon.

Miss Ruth Harrison whose toilet of black satin was relieved by a touch of ermine.

An hour of agreeable intercourse will follow this series of events, the membership being all cocked and primed to stay on to enjoy it.

Last but not least were the paragraphs which, puzzle as Cincinnatians would over them, not one ever knew what she meant:

In nothing to the Philistines are the May Festivals more intriguing than in the boxes and the Audience. Last night these themes of and corridor and foyer were paramount to the carnal-minded devotee of these two yearly events.

Center Shot

Cowan and Hoffman, Western hunters, were dead shots and each hotly jealous of the other's prowess. Setting out together one day after deer, they separated in the woods, taking opposite sides of a ridge.

Almost immediately, Hoffman heard Cowan's rifle fired off. He ran over to the spot, expecting to be obliged to help hang a deer. He found Cowan reloading but no deer carcass in sight. However, a startled calf was crashing off through the hazelnut bushes.

"Oh Lord!" Hoffman whooped with delight. "You didn't shoot at that calf, did you, hoss?"

"Suppose I did?" growled Cowan.

"Why'd you do a thing like that?"

"Took it for a deer."

"Don't look like you hit it."

"No — missed."

"How in the nation did that happen?"

"Wasn't just sure that it wasn't a calf."

"That," crowed Hoffman, "is what I call a pretty sorry hunter — to shoot at a calf for a deer, and miss it at that!"

"Don't be a fool," drawled Cowan, ramming home the charge in his rifle. "I shot at it just so as to hit it if it was a deer, and miss it if it was a calf."

Anonymous

Birth Denouncement

In our last week's issue we announced the birth of a son to Mr. and Mrs. Gilbert Parkinson. We regret any annoyance that this may have caused.

Indian Paper

Super Blunder

"Send Superman to Berlin!" During World War II this was probably the most ardent wish of little boys and followers of the Sunday comics. With America sending tons of men and material to faraway battlefields, why was it that the champion of truth, justice and the American way was languishing at home?

Super-surprisingly, it was because the man of steel was ruled 4-F by his draft board. Yes, in an ironic twist of fate that bordered on permanent suspension of disbelief, the nation's foremost fantasy hero had flunked his pre-induction physical! According to the funny papers, Superman's X-ray vision had betrayed him. Unwittingly he had seen *through* the army *eye* chart and had read the letters on another chart in the next room. Rejected, the super hero spent the war at home, peddling Red Cross and V-bonds.

Let Parents
Leave Well Enough Alone!

The small daughter of a famous surgeon always introduced herself, when asked her identity, as "Dr. Baker's daughter." Her mother decided to correct her, on the ground that it sounded too snobbish. "After this," said her mother, "just refer to yourself as Mary Baker."

Several days later a colleague of the physician leaned over and asked, "Aren't you Dr. Baker's little girl?"

"I always thought I was," answered the little girl. "But Mother says not."

Speak to Me of Love

He smiled and let his gaze fall to hers, so that her cheek began to glow. Ecstatically she waited until his mouth slowly neared her own. She knew only one thing: rdoeniadtrdgoveniardgoverdgov-nrdgog

Badische Presse

The vagaries of medical science give rise to some really rib-tickling blunders. As an example, here are a few letters to doctors collected by Juliet Lowell.

Dear Doctor

Bureau of Vital Statistics
New York City

Gentlemen:
In reply to your question, our death rate is the same here as elsewhere — 1 death for every inhabitant.

Dept. of Health
New York City

Dr. Endre A. Balazs
Institute of Biological & Medical Science
Boston

Dear Dr. Balazs,
I admire you and the work of your foundation so much that I am sending you this large donation. The reason my check is unsigned is to keep my husband from knowing what I'm doing.

Mrs. Alvin H_____

Cheating has always plagued Nevada gambling halls. In 1973, Newsweek *printed this item on a gambler whose blundering boots betrayed him.*

These Boots Ain't Made for Walkin'

One blackjack dealer recently got into the habit of palming silver dollars from the table and dropping them into his cowboy boots. After a long session of cards, he got up for a break — and discovered that he could hardly walk. Suspicious casino authorities made him take off his boots and turn them upside down. More than 200 silver dollars clattered onto the floor.

Is This Any Way to Run a War?

One hour before the attack on Pearl Harbor, army radar reported unidentified objects moving in. "Hell," said one officer, "it's probably just a pigeon with a metal band around its leg."

The picayune niceties of etiquette are responsible for many a faux pas. Consider the case of these hapless White House guests.

Table Manners

Ever been to a White House dinner? Few of us have. It's an occasion certainly for one to mind one's p's and q's. This same thought was on the minds of several Vermont friends of Calvin Coolidge as they dined one night with the President. The dinner passed uneventfully until coffee was served, and President Coolidge poured his into a saucer. Eager to please, the guests did the same. Then Coolidge added cream and sugar. The visitors did likewise. Then Coolidge leaned over and gave his to the cat.

Howard Lindsay tells this incredible story involving an actor, a rooster and the top brass of Hollywood's Pathé film company. Is this a plot or is this a plot!

Bird Thou Never Wert

Metro-Goldwyn-Mayer got the jump on all the others by having the lion in its trademark roar.

Only one other film had an animal as its trademark and that was the rooster of Pathé. It is not surprising that the heads of Pathé were determined to compete with Metro; they felt that it would be wonderful if their pictures started with a live rooster throwing back his head and uttering a triumphal cock-a-doodle-doo.

They made their plans. They got a handsome rooster from a man who rented out animals to picture firms, and considered the problem of photographing him as he crowed. It is well known that roosters crow at dawn, so the solution seemed simple. They telephoned the weather bureau in Washington to find out when it would be dawn the next day in Los Angeles. They were told it would be at 4:47.

The crew was called to the studio at 4:00 A.M. The rooster had his feet fixed to a small board with electricians' tape, and he was lighted with great care. The microphone was hung just over his head. Everyone was ready by 4:45. They held their breaths for the next two minutes. But when 4:47 came, and with it the dawn, the rooster was quite unaware of it. His inability to move his feet had made him indignant, and the heat of the lamps had made him unhappy; so he just sulked.

There followed a conference. One of the group, who had been born on a farm, assured the others that if one rooster heard another rooster crow he would crow in answer. But how to get the other rooster to crow? "That wouldn't be necessary," the country boy answered. There was an actor well known in Hollywood who imitated the sounds of animals. He was very good at it. All the studios had used him at one time or another. They would have him crow to the rooster who was representing Pathé and the Pathé rooster would crow in answer to him. So simple!

To ensure the success of this it was decided it had better be done again at dawn the following day. Again they telephoned Washington to make sure of the exact time. Again the crew was called for four o'clock. So was the actor who imitated animals. They had a rehearsal. What they felt was necessary was that the rooster should be able to hear this imitation cockcrow but that it shouldn't be picked up on the microphone. The animal imitator was placed farther and farther away from the microphone. The result was not successful until they opened the studio doors and had him out on the sidewalk. When he crowed from the sidewalk everyone including the rooster would hear him, but the microphone wouldn't pick up his voice. The rooster, strapped to his board, was brought in, he was carefully lighted, and the cameras focused.

This was all worked out ten or fifteen minutes before the time of dawn, so there was a hiatus before the magic moment. The actor used this time to rehearse. As dawn approached they turned to signal the actor out on the sidewalk but he was not in sight. They ran out to get his attention and bring him back to his designated spot, but he was nowhere to be seen. There was a search of the neighborhood but he had completely disappeared. The Pathé rooster again had failed to respond to the time of dawn and everyone was dismissed.

The head of the studio was very downhearted and went home to bed. He didn't turn up at his office that day until close to noon. There were the usual telephone messages for him, including one from the chief of police, whose call he returned. The chief said, "I wish you would straighten out something for me. Early this morning one of our squad cars picked up a man who was out on the street crowing like a rooster. He's been telling our psychiatrist that you hired him to do this. Is this true, and can you explain it to me?"

"Yes, it's true," the Pathé executive answered, "but I won't explain it." He just wasn't going to try. He was too discouraged. Neither he nor the rooster did any crowing.

Absentminded Professor

Although a giant in the world of physics, Albert Einstein never quite understood the priorities of the work-a-day world. He was, in fact, the original absentminded professor, innocent and childlike at heart. Mrs. Einstein had to mind him constantly lest he wander off in his bedroom slippers instead of galoshes. But even wifely supervision failed on the occasion when a philanthropic foundation sent him a check for $1,000. Albert used the check as a bookmark. Then he lost the book.

A jumble sale will be held in the Parish Room on Saturday 27th September. This is a chance to get rid of anything that is not worth keeping but is too good to throw away. Don't forget to bring your husbands.

St. Ambrose Parish Magazine

It's 10 P.M.
Do You Know Where Your Pigeons Are?

Twenty thousand homing pigeons were entered in the North Road Federation of Pigeon Fancier's annual race; 19,500 disappeared somewhere along the 150-mile course in Yorkshire, England.

In the world of blunders, as in everything else, there are sins of commission and omission. The sportswriters of America were certainly guilty of the latter when they failed to check out the story on Plainfield Teachers.

The Team That Never Was

Far above New Jersey's swamplands,
Plainfield Teachers' spires
Mark a phantom, phony college
That got on the wires.

Perfect record made on paper,
Imaginary team!
Hail to thee, our ghostly college,
Product of a dream!

A group of Wall Street brokers, with time heavy on their hands, once perpetrated a classic gag on the newspapers, a gag which was exposed only after considerable investigation into the whereabouts of Plainfield Teachers — unbeaten and untied in six games of the 1941 season (although there's no such place or no such team and never was). The brokers had been reporting the scores of this phantom institution of learning to newspapers all autumn, and the New York *Herald Tribune,* the *Times,* the *Post,* and the Associated Press accepted the information, dutifully printed it, and eventually longed for more news about John Chung, "stellar Chinese halfback" for Plainfield Teachers.

This modern version of Joel Sayre's Rackety Rax was the brainchild of a few stockbrokers at Newburger, Loeb & Co. who were wondering one day how such places as Slippery Rock got their scores into the newspapers. This led to the founding of Plainfield Teachers in the hope that dear old P.T. could get some space, too. The brokers took turns calling the papers on Saturday afternoon to report new victories for the team — and then gleefully awaited the Sunday editions. They even had a Philadelphia outlet, which hoodwinked the *Record* — and the leak finally came from there. At least, that's what they believed after they had been tracked down and made to come clean.

The leak reached *Time* Magazine, which carried an item on the gag. The brokers tried unsuccessfully to talk *Time's* editors out of printing it. When they knew the jig — or gag — was up they sent out one last publicity release and then had the one telephone at Plainfield Teachers disconnected.

The last publicity blurb, sent out by a press agent, was to the effect that because of a phalanx of flunkings in the mid-term examinations, Plainfield Teachers was forced to call off its last two scheduled games, with Appalachian Tech, November 15, and with Harmony Teachers, Thanksgiving Day.

"Among those thrown for a loss at examination time was John Chung, stellar Chinese halfback of the team who has accounted for 69 of Plainfield's 117 points," the blurb read. Plainfield, according to the record, had trampled successively on Scott, Chesterton, Winona, Randolph Tech, Ingersoll and St. Joseph. And Appalachian was to be stifled, 20-2, and Harmony was to put up a great game but succumb to Chung's wizardry, 40-27.

When the hoax was thriving, Herb Allan in the *Post* printed a glowing piece about Chung's exploits and the brokers decided that they needed a publicity man and a telephone. They invented the name Jerry Croyden for the tub thumper, and had a phone installed in Morris Newburger's office. The telephone service cost five dollars.

After the exposé there were suspicions that a betting coup was involved in the scheme, but there was no such thing. Plainfield Teachers wasn't a money-maker; it was just plain fun. When the cultured voice of "Jerry Croyden" called a newspaper and gave the score of the Randolph Tech game (35-0), the rewrite man asked where Randolph Tech was.

"Delaware," was the prompt reply. "Wilmington?" queried the rewrite man. "No, just outside," said Jerry Croyden.

Sir Walter Raleigh, He's Not

It was a wet day in Southern California and the pavement in front of Keystone was half an inch deep in mud and water. Chester Conklin spied Mable (Normand) across the street, wondering how to get across, and made a fancy gesture. He bowed like a headwaiter expecting a fifty-dollar tip, snatched off his coat, and spread it in the mud for Mabel to step on. She stepped, and disappeared into a manhole.

Mack Sennett

As the inimitable baseball great Dizzy Dean once said, "I know the King's English — so's the Queen!" But for those who have only a nodding acquaintance with our native tongue, the king's English can prove something of an embarrassment. Here are some idioms and idiosyncrasies from the collection of traveller Nino Lo Bello.

Gaining a Little Humor
in the Translation

English has become the world's common language (now that more than a billion people have a working acquaintance with it), but the king's English can turn into Le Joke Hilarious when it comes from someone for whom English is not the mother tongue. Everybody seems to be popping out with signs in windows which will tell you for your benefit that "Here Speeching English," "American Pronounced" or "English Goodly Spocken."

Some old pros in the tourist business seem to have studied the English language in order to cater to the annual avalanche of travelers who lug their dollars with them to the Continent. All fine and dandy — but more often than not, restaurant and hotel keepers who mean well when they put up a notice or write down a menu don't quite get it keerect, alas. Here's what one hotel here in Zurich told clients:

"Because of the impropriety of entertaining guests of the opposite sex in the bedroom, it is suggested that the lobby be used for this purpose."

Or the Rome hotel which wants to warn guests about the fire regulations. On every floor is the following:

"Fire! It is what can doing we hope. No fear. Not ourselves. Say quietly to all people coming up down everywhere a prayer. Always is a clerk. He is assured of safety by expert men who are in the bar for telephone for the fighters of the fire come out."

That flip of the tongue is reminiscent of the Italian doctor up the block with his sign proclaiming him a "Specialist in Women and Other Diseases."

Inevitably tourist brochures suffer from the maime-English-syndrome, too. Prospective visitors to Poland are told that "as for the tripe served you at the Hotel Monopol, you will be singing its praises to your grandchildren as you lie on your deathbed."

Not to be outdone by their Communist brethren, the Soviets are guilty of the following sin-tax found tacked on a Moscow hotel room door: "If this is your first visit to the U.S.S.R., you are welcome to it."

Even the British (who are sometimes known to speak English themselves) muff one occasionally, as witness a hospital sign in London that reads: "Visitors. Two to A Bed and Half-an-Hour Only." Blimey, if it isn't the English who are also responsible for this linguistic lapse: "Our Establishment Serves Tea In A Bag Like Mother."

Discovered in a small Ionian Sea hotel, which doesn't supply dictionary facilities, was this beaut of a bobble: "To all Hotel assistants, in order to prevent shoes from misleying, please don't corridor them. The Management of the Hotel cannot be held. He is responsible for articles deposited to the office against receipt."

Then there is the dentist in Istanbul whose doorway proclaims: "American Dentist, 2th Floor — Teeth Extracted By Latest Methodists."

What makes his sign particularly delightful (and it gets the grand prize!) is that the second floor would be pronounced, according to this particular dentist, "tooth floor."

One hotel in France, seeking to discourage Americans from wearing slacks to its plush dining room, informs men that "A sports jacket may be worn to dinner but no trousers." That same hotel, eager to put on airs and preferring not to call an egg an egg, pretentiously lists an egg on their menu as "extract of fowl, peached or sunside up."

Boners and blunders are self-perpetuating. This is Wood's law. One begets the other. Take the case of the young blunderbuss dubbed "Wrong-way Corrigan." On July 18, 1938 he took off for a transcontinental flight from New York to Los Angeles. On July 19 he found himself in Dublin, Ireland. Afflicted with terminal under-statement, Corrigan said, "It sure does show what a bum navigator a guy can be." But I said blunders are self-perpetuating. The second blun-der was that the world clamored to make Corri-gan an airline pilot. Heavens! I can see it now. "This is your captain speaking. There will be a slight delay in your regularly scheduled Seattle to Cleveland flight. Meanwhile, welcome to Gnome, Alaska."

Hello, Where Am I?

Stoutly maintaining that he was "real embar-rassed" when he found he had flown to Ireland, Douglas G. Corrigan explained in his soft, pleas-ant voice yesterday that he had thought all the time he was heading for California, but that he had made a mistake in setting the dial of his compass.

"I'm sure ashamed of that navigation, all right," he said.

...The Columbia Broadcasting System carried an interview with him, while the National Broadcasting Company broadcast a two-way conversation between the flier in Dublin and his uncle and grandmother in Hollywood, Calif.

"I don't use any flight maps, so I fly across the right number of hours to get there, then look to see if I'm there." Corrigan said in explanation of his method of navigation. This time, he said, he had figured out a course from New York to Los Angeles, "and then just changed the course about once an hour to make a sort of circle out of it."

When he decided it was time to come down, he said, the first thing he saw was water, then a couple of fishing boats, and then a coast which "didn't look right." He followed the coast until he came to the first big city, Dublin, where he landed.

"I was real embarrassed," he remarked. "It sure does show what a bum navigator a guy can be."...

Corrigan said that he had at one time wanted to fly to Europe, but that he abandoned that idea last year. "Now I'm here without any idea," he added....

Asked whether he would return home in his plane, Corrigan, who seemed to take the whole affair as a good joke, said in his soft drawl:

"Oh, no. It'll probably be in a boat. I don't know.

That's going to be kind of risky. I was never over a lot of water in a boat before."

"What sort of a sensation did you get when you discovered you weren't flying toward Los Angeles at all?" the interviewer asked.

"Well, I came down and saw the water, so I looked at the compass and found out that I had set the dial wrong so it was all my fault," he replied.

In his conversation with his 92-year-old grandmother, and his uncle and aunt, the Rev. and Mrs. S. Frazier Langford, Corrigan told them that "I guess you were surprised by this flight, but then, so was I."

The announcer intervened to say that Mrs. Langford was worried about his meeting "some of those beautiful French girls," and Mrs. Langford herself came on the air to urge him to "wait until you get back and get an American girl."

"I'll fool you, I won't get any," Corrigan replied.

His grandmother came to the microphone and said she hoped he would soon be home.

"We miss you," she went on. "Don't you try to fly back. Come back by boat. Come back by boat. Did you hear? Come back by boat."

New York Times
July 19, 1938

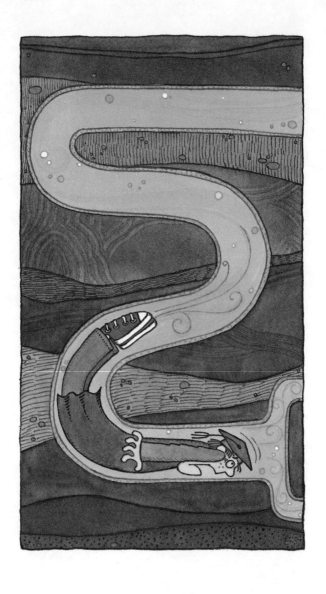

Let the Punishment Fit the Crime

Mr. Firestone argued that his client was a student, had not been found guilty, and should not be sub-hauled by tank steamer to the east coast, and then pumped back into the middle-west and the Great Lakes area through pipe-lines.

Cleveland Press

Der Dufferblunder

Riding high as the reigning Masters and U.S. Open Champion, Arnold Palmer came apart on the ninth hole of the 1961 Los Angeles Open. It was a par five. Arnold made it in twelve. Two 3-wood shots went out of bounds to the right; two went out of bounds to the left. Now there's a plaque there to commemorate the fiasco.